Horrible, No-Good, Lousy, F*#%ing Bosses and How Not to Be One

Short Stories of Leadership Nightmares and the Things We Can Learn

R. Torres

Copyright © 2024 Richard Torres

All rights reserved

No part of this book may be reproduced, stored in a retrieval system, or transmitted in any form or by any means, electronic, mechanical, photocopying, recording, or otherwise, without the express written permission of the publisher.

Cover illustration created using OpenAI's DALL-E.

ISBN: 9798326739773
Imprint: Independently published

DEDICATION

To my wife, my children, and my family, who inspire, support, tolerate, and love me through it all.

To my mentor, Captain Mike Redding, who inspired me by once asking, "God has given you an opportunity; now, what are you going to do with it?"

CONTENTS

DEDICATION..iii

PREFACE 6

PROLOGUE 8

CHAPTER 1..11

"Miriam and The Curse of Rock-Paper-Scissors" 11

    Let's talk about all the ways Miriam sucked. 17

    What does this mean to you?..18

    Key Takeaways 19

CHAPTER 2..21

"Erik and the Case of the Muddy Mop"......................................21

    Let's talk about all the ways Erik sucked. 34

    What does this mean to you?..35

    Key Takeaways 38

CHAPTER 3..40

"Bert Was a Dick"...40

    Let's talk about all the ways Bert sucked. 47

    What does this mean to you?..47

    Key Takeaways 50

CHAPTER 4..53

"Tom - the Global Everything"...53

    Let's talk about ~~all~~ *some* of the ways Tom sucked 66

    What does this mean to you?..67

Key Takeaways	69
CHAPTER 5	71
Let's Talk About You	71
ACKNOWLEDGEMENTS	80
AFTERWORD	81

PREFACE

If you're reading this, you likely fall into one of three categories: 1. You've suffered under a horrible boss and are determined not to follow in those footsteps, 2. You possess an odd sense of humor and enjoy reading about terrible leaders, or 3. You are a horrible boss—perhaps this book was a gift (hint, hint), or you've recognized the need for change and are here for help. Regardless of your reasons, I'm glad you're here, and I hope these stories resonate with you meaningfully.

"Horrible, No-Good, Lousy..." was initially a form of therapy for me, born out of both personal experiences and those I witnessed that showcased shocking examples of leadership at its worst. When I first shared these tales, many thought they were exaggerated for effect. Rest assured, no exaggeration is necessary; the reality was unsettling enough on its own.

As more people shared their own horror stories with me, the idea for this book took root. The final nudge came when, after quipping to my wife and a close friend about writing a book on disastrous bosses, they both encouraged me, saying, "Do it. I have tons of stories you can put in your book." It turns out terrible leadership is sadly quite common.

These experiences aren't unique. However, I aim to create a unique approach to leadership training by shining a light on the darker side of leadership and converting lessons for those aspiring to lead better. I hope this book becomes a crucial part of your leadership journey, inspiring you to learn from the worst and strive to be your best.

PROLOGUE

Picture this: You walk into work on a Monday morning, already dreading the encounter with your boss. As you step into the conference room, you overhear a conversation that sends a chill down your spine. "I don't have time for people's personal bullshit," your boss snaps about a new employee. This single sentence sums up the toxic environment you endure daily.

Hundreds, nay, thousands of quality books have been written on leadership, all claiming to share the fundamentals, the laws, key principles, irrefutable attributes, and secrets that will change your life forever. This book takes a slightly different approach. Don't get me wrong, those books adorn my shelves, and their lessons have helped me become the leader I am today. I highly recommend many of them and have even bought them for leaders I was mentoring; know ahead of time that you may also want to send this book to a very different audience, namely the assholes this book reminds you of.

In this book, you'll meet a gallery of such bosses – the ones who crush morale, stifle creativity, and make you question your career choices. These are not ordinary bad managers; these are the horror stories worthy of a reality TV show. You know the type – the ones who get away with murder. Not the literal kind, of course, but the kind that kills morale, trust, happiness, creativity, collaboration, freedom of expression, work-life balance, and even productivity. These bosses do this so frequently they could be considered serial killers of workplace morale.

If you've ever seen the movie "Casino," think of that bar scene with Joe Pesci and the pen. That's what these bosses are doing to morale in the workplace. They are the selfish, egomaniacal, manipulative, creepy, horrible, no-good, lousy f*#%ing bosses that drive you to share stories on social media or at dinner parties about how impressively awful they are.

Through these stories, you will see the dark side of leadership – the ego-driven decisions, the petty grievances, the manipulation, and the sheer incompetence that turns workplaces into battlegrounds. But there's a silver lining. By exposing these nightmare bosses, this book aims to shed light on what true leadership should not be.

As you turn the pages, you might find glimpses

of your own experiences or perhaps see reflections of your own behavior. This book is not just about pointing fingers; it's about learning, growing, and striving to be better. If you see yourself in these stories, take it as a wake-up call. Acknowledging the problem is the first step toward change.

So, dive in, and prepare to be both horrified and enlightened. Let these cautionary tales guide you toward becoming the leader who inspires, rather than the boss who is feared. And remember, if you ever catch yourself acting like one of these dreadful bosses, stop, reflect, and choose a different path, or end up being just another no-good, lousy boss.

CHAPTER 1

"Miriam and The Curse of Rock-Paper-Scissors"

One of my earliest bad boss experiences was while working in a juvenile treatment facility for at-risk youth. My role was to provide daily oversight, guidance, and behavioral coaching for a dozen or so teenage and pre-teen males in a residential setting. Rest assured, if this sounds like a glorified babysitter job, that's because it was.

My daily tasks were enforcing house rules, leading activities, and trying to keep these boys from setting the place on fire. I guided them through routine chores like cooking, cleaning, laundry, and yard work, and even helped with homework when I wasn't searching for contraband or breaking up fights. There was no formal training for this job, no written guidance, little in the way of positive reinforcement, and even fewer enforceable consequences to address misbehavior. There is a rumor that fruit roll-ups and extra TV time may have been used occasionally to reward good behavior - if you're a parent, you get it.

One evening, the boys were particularly defiant after a scuffle broke out over an extra cup of pudding or something equally insignificant. I was on duty with two other colleagues, and we were beyond frustrated with both the terrible behaviors and our lack of skills to address them. We had exhausted almost every tactic and technique we could think of. Still, time and again, our efforts were met with colorful language, creative hand gestures, and suggestions to perform some unnatural acts on ourselves. At our wit's end, we began discussing calling our boss for additional guidance.

Calling for help was no easy decision to make as we each had emotional scars from our experiences of calling she who shall be named "Miriam". Most phone calls were met with ridicule, scorn, and a healthy dose of shame for not knowing the correct answers instinctively. To remind us that our calls to her were unwelcome, Miriam used to eliminate the courtesy of saying goodbye. Most calls ended with one of us in mid-sentence interrupted by the tone of a disconnected call. This call, however, wasn't a simple question about policy or procedure; we were calling to report an escalating crisis that could have led to a 911 call if unchecked.

Did I already mention that it was a Saturday evening? Not only were we about to call someone who disliked us during regular business hours, but we were about to do it on her day off. This led to a heated debate over who she liked best (or, rather, who she disliked the least) and who should be the one to make the actual call. On one thing, we all agreed: she disliked all of us, and there was no favorite. To resolve our dilemma of who would make the call, we engaged in a sophisticated, scientific, chance-based, randomized selection process: rock-paper-scissors. As you might imagine - I begged for the best two out of three but was immediately dismissed after squarely losing to each of my peers.

While my peers were unwilling to make the call in my stead, they did help me practice what I was going to say. The call had to be short and specific, and I had to be sure I was prepared for any questions she asked. There was a lot of second-guessing and questioning ourselves, but things were still getting out of hand, and we knew it was just a matter of time before someone got hurt.

With sweaty palms and me actively questioning my life choices, I initiated the call. Even before the phone rang, I started praying to hear the sounds of an answering machine. Fate is a fickle bitch, Miriam answered on the first ring as if she kept the phone beside her cauldron where she boiled baby kittens with eye of newt. There was no hello, only a "yesss" that sounded eerily like "your mother is ashamed of you." She always knew when a call was coming from the facility as the new technology of the day worked against us, caller ID.

Through my fear, I explained the situation as best I could over the odd sounds from the other end of the phone – tones of heavy, labored breathing interrupted by what can only be described as a sort of growling. There was no verbal response from Miriam, only a very distinctive and anticipated "click." A few thoughts crossed my mind: "Should I call back?" "Am I fired?" "Should I sharpen some wooden stakes?"

The next half hour was spent facing the ongoing jeers of the facility's youth and fighting to ignore comments like "Oh, I see you needed to call your mommy." While we felt helpless, we were frustrated because we were left powerless. There was no plan for dealing with a situation like ours. We ignored the comments and reassured each other that asking for help when needed was the right thing to do. We went so far as to convince ourselves that we would be praised for being proactive rather than waiting for things to continue to escalate (we were all young and still very naive).

A knock at the front door caused a hush to fall on the house's occupants. My peer opened the door and let in our boss, who stormed past us like a raging bull without so much as a sneer or even simple eye contact. She entered the great room and immediately addressed the youth who stood poised, ready for a confrontation.

I thought, "This is it; boy, are they gonna get it. After this tongue-lashing, they'll think twice before openly defying us again." Much to our surprise, she did not bring down the wrath of Miriam as we predicted. Instead, she addressed them as though they were the victims of some abuse or tragic event at our hands. We were the villains, and she was there to support them in their hour of need.

My peers and I watched in equal parts disbelief and outrage as she huddled them closely and apologized for our behaviors and lack of professionalism. Then, she delivered the killing blow by granting them an extra hour of television for the evening. She said her goodbyes to the boys, pivoted on her left hoof and walked right past us again as she headed for the exit, only this time, she offered a dirty look and grunt that escaped the curl in her snarled lip. An awkward silence after she slammed the door would have been welcomed and undoubtedly preferable to the jeers and laughter directed at me and my peers for the next three hours until the night shift staff arrived.

In the days that followed our betrayal, we were all individually counseled for our inability to maintain order and enforce the house rules. We returned to work in humiliation, were taunted to our faces, and were rendered utterly ineffective in our roles, with no credibility or backing from our boss. This was not the first time Miriam failed to support us, but it was certainly the last time for me, as I resigned a few days later. Two things happened that day. First, I promised that I would never be the type of leader who abandoned my troops in need, and second, I vowed never to rely on rock-paper-scissors to make a potentially career-altering decision ever again.

Let's talk about all the ways Miriam sucked.

Starting with the obvious:

- Her employees were afraid to ask for help or guidance
- Dealing with her employees was treated as an inconvenience
- She treated the people she was supposed to be leading with disrespect and contempt

Several overt and subtle behaviors contributed to the poor morale and dysfunctional environment Miriam created.

- Miriam had a terrible habit of using disparaging phrases such as:
    - "I'm the boss."
    - "Not sure why you thought that was a good idea."
    - "Do I just need to do your job for you?"
- Miriam behaved as though she was above the common courtesy and pleasantries that are the social norms that most of us subscribe to, such as saying hello and goodbye or not walking away from someone while they were still talking.

- After providing guidance or coaching to someone, she would typically make sarcastic and snide comments that made people feel shame or guilt.

What does this mean to you?

Miriam, in my opinion, was a genuinely unlikeable person, but that isn't what made her lousy. I've respected and followed many people I didn't like personally. However, when a boss routinely comes across as rude, smug, and condescending, employees can become anxious and resentful, among other things, none of which are productive or serve to build people up.

Teams can, however, survive a terrible boss like Miriam. To do so, the team would need enough leadership within the ranks to counter the horrible boss's crap, or the team would have to have been well-established before a Miriam-type came along to crush them. Remember, when a person's fight-or-flight response is triggered, they perceive a threat. Fight-or-flight emotions are never something a real leader wants their people to feel.

Key Takeaways

Words have impact. I can't think of a good reason to use the phrase "I'm the boss" unless it's followed by, "...therefore I take full responsibility." Be conscientious and reflect on what you say, even when you think you're being cute; your words may be hurtful or harmful and alienate the people you're supposed to embrace, even if said in jest. There's a fine line between being funny and being a d*%k. Don't be a d*%k.

Courtesy and respect are non-negotiable. Not treating people with courtesy and respect conveys a powerful message. It tells people they are not worth your time and not worth your consideration. Good leaders don't have to be overly pleasant or even charming. I've known many strong leaders who were very matter-of-fact. However, to amount to anything more than just a boss (essentially a leader in title or position only), you have to care about how you impact people's self-esteem (how they feel about themselves), self-image (how they see themselves in relation to others), and self-worth (how they believe they are valued). Don't walk on eggshells or spend an unrealistic amount of time worrying about bruising fragile egos, but do treat people like people first, not just workers.

Building up and supporting people IS the job. If you are unwilling to invest your time and provide the guidance and support necessary to the people who rely on you, don't accept a leadership role PERIOD. Consider that you may be one of those people who add value to an organization as an individual contributor. Without the willingness (more importantly, the desire) to build up the people around you, you'll resent your people for needing you. You'll never be more than a boss (and likely a pretty f*#%ing lousy one at that). Captain Mike used to say, "The only reason you're here is for them."

CHAPTER 2

"Erik and the Case of the Muddy Mop"

Some stories of bad leadership draw strong reactions and comments from people, such as, "No way that happened," "How do they still have a job?" or "How did this person ever get into a leadership role?". Few of my bosses drew as many of those reactions as Erik. While the mop was the final straw, I've broken the story into 3 parts to provide more backstory. (I thought about telling the story and then writing a prequel, but that seems a bit overdone – thanks, Geroge Lucas.)

Part 1 – The Job Posting

Once again, I found myself working in a juvenile justice program. This time, I was a team lead at a high-security juvenile treatment center, gaining valuable leadership experience in a very structured environment. I came to work one Monday morning, punched the time clock (if you don't know what an actual time clock is, Google it), and looked over the bulletin board for any new announcements or reminders for the week. I immediately noticed a job posting for the Operations

Manager position. The posting caught me by surprise since I shared an office with the Ops Manager, a gentleman we'll call Fred, and he had never mentioned anything about leaving.

I entered the office, spotted Fred at his desk, said good morning, and asked, "So Fred, you're leaving us?"

Without taking his eyes off his work, Fred replied, "It would appear so." There was both sarcasm and disgust in his voice, and it was written all over his face.

I probed further, "are you taking a new position," I asked cautiously.

Fred offered a monotone and stoic response, "Don't really know. I just walked in and saw that my job was posted this morning."

Instant regret. I had created a very awkward moment and needed an excuse to leave. I said something stupid like, "I'm going to grab some coffee. Do you want some?" It was stupid because Fred didn't drink coffee, and I knew that. Fred knew I knew it and lifted his eyes long enough to let me know. Since there was very little I could do to make it worse, I just walked out to wash down the foot now lodged in my mouth.

Down the hall, I spotted my supervisor, Mitchell, talking with the Program Director, whom we'll call "Erik." Erik was everyone's boss at the facility, but Fred reported to him directly. I walked over and waited for an opening to bring up my recent awkward moment. They could both tell I had something to say because I'm sure I was still visibly uncomfortable. I was finally able to share my encounter and quickly noticed a confused look on Mitchell's face, followed by a visible change in Erik's demeanor. Erik asked with a chilled tone, "The posting is on the board?"

"Yes," I replied.

Erik began shaking his head as if in disbelief, and then Erik said something I didn't expect. He closed his eyes and said, "dammit, Torres, of course, <u>you</u> had to go and say something to him."

Caught squarely by surprise, I said, "All I did was ask him about it. Fred had obviously seen it before I said a word." None of that seemed to matter.

Erik turned and walked to the threshold of his office, then turned back as he stared down toward the floor with his eyes darting left and right. After a brief moment, he spoke, "Torres, the laundry room was left unlocked last night. I'm having Mitchell write you up." Erik then turned, entered his office, and shut the door passionately.

Erik's words landed on my ears but didn't make sense, as if they were gibberish. I looked at Mitchell, intending to ask a WTF question (and no, that isn't the World TaeKwonDo Federation). By the expression of bewilderment on his face, I instantly knew that he was caught off guard.

Mitchell looked at me and must have known what I was thinking. He held his hands up in submission and said, "Dude, I have no idea. Let me go find out what the f*#k that was about."

As it turned out, HR posted the position, as instructed by Erik the week before. Erik had procrastinated and never got around to telling Fred he was being let go before it got posted for everyone to see. As for the laundry room, one of my staff members failed to lock the laundry room door during the previous night shift, which was a well-known expectation. Much to Mitchell's dismay and mine, Mitchell had no choice but to issue me a disciplinary counseling statement because of my "lack of leadership and oversight" – despite the fact that I had been on vacation until that very morning.

Part 2 – The Dirt Pile

Corporate leaders were flying in from out of town for a facility tour. The entire staff had come in over the weekend to clean up, make last-minute repairs, and decorate for their arrival. The visitors arrived around noon, observed classroom activities, watched us run the students (referred to as "cadets") through some daily activities, and stayed until just around dinner time. When the visit was done, they said their goodbyes and shook hands with the staff, thanking them for their efforts. One of the corporate directors placed his hand on my shoulder and waved to Erik to get his attention. When Erik looked over, the gentleman asked, pointing at me, "This is Mr. Torres, correct?"

Erik replied, "Yes sir, that's him," as he walked over, giving me a look that clearly expressed his displeasure. At what exactly, I wasn't sure; the entire day went off without a hitch, but I knew it wouldn't be anything good, nonetheless.

The gentlemen shook my hand firmly and said, "Mr. Torres, I've gotten a great deal of positive feedback about you today from both cadets and staff. Sounds like you're adding a great deal of value here." His compliments shocked me since they were scarce from our local leadership. I had just assumed that our local office culture reflected the corporate culture, and I was pleasantly surprised.

Weeks before this event, I attended a martial arts seminar held by some guys who frequented the cover of Black Belt Magazine. There was a slew of personalities there, mostly self-promoting, egocentric bull-shitters spinning tall tales of their legendary accomplishments. However, what stood out to me was the humility and gentle manner of some of the most senior experts. They shied away from the groupies and attention hounds and, when approached, cared more about me and my background than retelling their own stories. When pressed, they were quick to talk about all the people who helped them learn and grow as martial artists and people. I took a hard lesson from that experience and reflected on how often I recognized those around me. That experience was still fresh in my head while this gentleman complimented me.

I listened carefully as the director continued his exchange with Erik. I couldn't help but notice that Erik never actually agreed with the man; instead, he talked about himself. When they were done, I expressed my gratitude for his words but quickly credited the great team I had around me.

The director then asked me, "Are you tied to this area, or would you consider relocating if there was an opportunity for you?"

Out of the corner of my eye, I could barely make out the look on Erik's face. I didn't want to look directly at him, but I knew it wasn't a look of pride. I informed the director that I would have to confer with my wife but would certainly be willing to discuss it. He looked at Erik and said, "I hate to do that to you, Erik, but we need to spread the talent around." Erik just smiled and nodded.

The guests were escorted out of the facility, and the staff all made their way back to the main building to celebrate the day. Erik called me over before I entered the building. He escorted me to where Mitchell was talking to another staff member by a picnic table. "Mitchell, you remember me telling Torres to make sure the admin building was squared away before everyone arrived," Erik asked with a stern look on his face.

Mitchell looked over at me, then at the staff member he was speaking to, before replying, "Mr. Torres was here until after midnight last night making sure it was all done."

Erik was not happy with his answer and snapped back at him, "That's not what I asked you."

Mitchell looked quite put off by the comment and modified his response. "Yes, I remember you telling …"

Erik interrupted before Mitchell could finish his statement, "There's a pile of dirt by the back door of the admin building. I'm gonna need you to go ahead and write Mr. Torres up for that." Erik then turned and walked away. None of us said anything until he was back inside the building with the door shut behind him.

Mitchell and I had seen this act only a month or so earlier regarding the laundry room, but we still didn't quite know how to react. As I prepared to ask my usual "WTF" question, the staff member standing with us spoke up. "Umm, guys, that was me. I swept up after everyone tracked dirt into the building just after breakfast. I went to get a dustpan and just forgot to go back and clean it up."

I interjected just before Mitchell had a chance to respond, "Thank you for doing that; I appreciate you taking the initiative. But, it was my responsibility to make sure it stayed squared away today." The young man appeared to be both relieved and slightly confused.

Mitchell ended up issuing me a disciplinary counseling statement for "failure to ensure task completion" or some bullshit like that. There was never any mention of the comments from that director or any follow-up. Part of me figured that Erik would do to me what I've seen him do to others he didn't like: speak harshly of me behind my back and likely ruin any potential opportunities he didn't approve of. In retrospect, Erik was the dirt pile that needed cleaning up.

Part 3 – The Muddy Mop

One of the expectations that a semi-retired facility director expressed on several occasions when the program first started was, "We work every day." "We don't take days off." That meant every Team Lead, Supervisor, or Manager was expected to go to the facility daily, regardless of their work schedule, family commitments, or even in some cases, travel plans.

I made my customary rounds on a typical Saturday afternoon, engaging with each staff member to see if they needed anything. An additional hand was often beneficial for the supervisor to coordinate breaks or gather essential supplies. When I arrived, the team members were deeply involved in various duties, from leading cadet activities and assisting with homework to handling weekend housekeeping responsibilities. One particular staff member was guiding a cadet through his chore of mopping a lengthy corridor.

Observing them, I noticed the mop and water had become quite grimy, with the mop spreading as much dirt as it was supposed to clean. Not wanting to disrupt the valuable teaching moment, I headed to the utility closet at the end of the hall, fetched a new mop, and filled a bucket with fresh water. This act reflected a principle my father instilled in me: "No task is too small, and the value lies in our work, not in our rank or title." I was confident that this principle, already embedded in our team's culture, would be underscored by the staff member in her guidance to the young man.

After delivering the fresh equipment, I returned the muddy stuff to the utility closet and began rinsing them to be stored for the next chore. Being one of those rare occasions that Erik actually showed up on a weekend, he strutted down the hall past the utility room and spotted me as I wrung out the mop. He offered a quick nod and a short, "Wa'sup, Torres?" I was in the middle of my response when I realized he had kept walking and couldn't actually hear me (and probably didn't genuinely care).

I arrived at the facility early Monday morning, said hello to some folks by the coffee maker, and went straight to my desk to get a head start on the mountain of paperwork that awaited. Minutes later, Mitchell walked into the office and sat at the desk adjacent to mine (Fred's old desk). After a few moments of sitting quietly, he broke the silence and said, "Hey, Mr. Torres, I've got this document here I need to share with you."

Still focused on my paperwork from the weekend, I just assumed it was some incident report or other document he had questions about. When I glanced up briefly, I noticed that the HR manager had come in with him. He continued, "So, you were caught in the utility room washing a dirty mop this weekend, so

I'm gonna have to give you this."

"Caught" seemed like a funny choice of words, and I immediately thought this was one of those "you were caught doing a good job" moments that my team used to do routinely for each other as recognition. I replied with a chuckle, "Caught huh?" Neither Mitchell nor the HR manager looked amused. Instead, they had a rather funny look on their face. Not a haha funny look, more of a "this is awkward" funny look.

"What's going on," I asked, still thinking this might be a lighthearted moment.

Mitchell held up the piece of paper he was referring to and said, "I'm really sorry. I need to go over this with you." I was no longer smiling.

I repeated what I thought I had heard, "I was caught cleaning a mop, is that right?"

Mitchell went on to tell me that this was my third offense and that I was being demoted back down to Associate (an entry-level position). I took his words in for a moment. Still thinking this was a gag, I responded with, "Okay, you got me. What's actually on the paper?"

"I'm serious. Erik said you weren't delegating and

had no business messing with muddy mops," Mitchell responded in a tone I hadn't heard from him before, one of sorrow. The HR manager didn't utter a single word or make eye contact.

My response was less than professional, "I'm being demoted...for washing a f*#%ing mop!" No one responded. I began to explain the circumstances of what I was doing and why but stopped midway as I realized what was happening. "This has nothing to do with a mop, does it?"

The room was silent. Neither Mitchell nor the HR manager could offer a single word of comfort or help me make sense of it. Mitchell spoke up after a very long silence, "Hold on a minute, don't do anything, this is not right, I'm not doing this." He stood up quickly and stormed out of the room with HR right on his heels. I sat there in disbelief, thinking, "There is no way this is happening." Something in me refused to believe that someone could be that petty and spiteful as to make up reasons to get rid of me. I was wrong.

Twenty minutes passed. I got up from my desk and walked out. My resignation letter was submitted that afternoon. I never spoke to Mitchell again, but I heard from former colleagues that he had left that position shortly after and moved back up north. As for Erik, he was eventually investigated and fired after he apparently "lost his shit" and threatened a female employee in front of witnesses. I left there having had many great experiences with a fantastic team, but I also took with me a valuable education on how not to underestimate just how spiteful and crooked a lousy f*#%ing boss can be.

Let's talk about all the ways Erik sucked.

This particular list could go on for several pages, but we'll focus on the top 3:

- Erik couldn't take ownership of his own mistakes and instead took them out on others
- Erik viewed positive feedback directed at his subordinates as a challenge to his position of importance
- Erik was vengeful and petty and used his authority as a weapon to instill fear and retaliate for perceived attacks on his ego.

Horrible, No-Good, Lousy, F*#%ing Bosses...

What does this mean to you?

Erik's ego was set to HIGH with the knob ripped off. He routinely said things like, "...back in the day, I was the best ____" and "Hey...did you see how I did that?" None of his braggart moments led to a teaching moment, making them all even harder to listen to after a while. We've all been conversing with people who interrupt or negate our story by saying things like, "That's nothing" or "Don't feel bad" just before they tell you why their experience trumps yours. Erik did that so often you could easily think there was some prize for who had the best or worst experiences, and he was the reigning champ in both weight classes.

I recall a few occasions when a co-worker received praise for something, and Erik developed this look of contempt on his face. When anyone would dare to try and address these behaviors, he would insist that it was everyone else "walking around in low-self," as he called it, referring to a person displaying signs of having low self-esteem. Erik also had a terrible habit of criticizing and disparaging people behind their backs. Rather than coaching and mentoring, he would smear them to their peers, which is poison to any work culture. If the boss talks to you about others, they'll talk to others about you. Ultimately, subordinates could neither relate to him, trust him or have room to feel good about themselves.

When in a position of leadership, you will have unique opportunities to impact people's lives in very meaningful ways. One such opportunity that should not be missed is the chance to build someone up with targeted and meaningful praise. Exceptional leaders have the ability to tell someone precisely what traits, behaviors, and talents they have that make them special, valued, and important. Never underestimate the power of meaningful praise.

As for the Job Offer, the Dirt Pile, and the Muddy Mop, it was clear that Erik accepted no ownership for his own mistakes and could not appreciate the people around him for who they were and what they contributed. A Real leader wants to celebrate the successes and accomplishments of their people and never seek out opportunities to minimize, insult, or arbitrarily discipline them to satisfy whatever emotional void they have inside. When a person lashes out at their people, they weaken any chance of creating a healthy environment based on trust and respect. These are amongst the very worst character traits to have as a leader, qualifying Erik as a horrible f*#%ing boss.

Key Takeaways

Take ownership. Recognize that everything happening is somehow tied back to you, no matter how small. When something goes wrong, taking full ownership sends a very clear message to those around you and creates a strong culture where excuses and blame are unacceptable.

Ego is the path to "Team Death." Ego is part of who we are, be it a lens through which our inner selves see the world around us or some other highly philosophical construct. Allowing an inflated ego, or one that is fragile and prone to hyper self-preservation, to drive behaviors and decision-making will always drive a wedge right through the heart of a team. Leadership roles are not established for focusing on and highlighting oneself, despite the characterization in film and television. As leaders, our ego is one equal ingredient to everyone else's. The less influence your ego has, the more room your team will have to grow and thrive. If you were to look back on the friendships, partnerships, and teams that lasted the longest and achieved the most, you would find that the team killer, ego, was always kept in check.

Authority misused is tyranny. Authority in leadership is built on trust. The nature of a role or position grants some decision-making power. However, the authority to make decisions related to people must be handled with the utmost care. Once a leader demonstrates the willingness to abuse their authority against others, not only have they crossed a very material line in their relationships with their people, but they will also always be seen as nothing more than a lousy, egotistical, f*#% n' boss – and rightfully so.

CHAPTER 3

"Bert Was a Dick"

Nope, no catchy title for this chapter. This boss was lousy, obnoxious, aloof, and insulting (I honestly believe that everyone who ever met him wanted to punch his stupid face at least once). I could fill several pages just listing examples of the overt and subtle behaviors that made this boss both ineffective and unlikable. Bert was one of those people who became a boss because he was intelligent, articulate, and had a critical eye for detail. While these are all valuable attributes you may look for in someone in charge of bookkeeping, they alone are not vital ingredients for being a good leader.

As a point of interest, I want to share that I had worked directly for Bert before this particular tale took place. Once the opportunity presented itself, I transferred out of that role to get away from him, but over the next few years, he seemed to follow me from one role to another like the proverbial bad penny. Hopefully, he now works in a cubical somewhere where he can't continue to piss off everyone around him.

Bert was left in charge for a week while our mutual, mostly lousy boss, Will, was on vacation. This usually meant that my peers and I were in for a week of micro-managing, criticism, and confusion, enough so that we were counting the days until our arrogant, lousy-ish boss returned. Taking accountability for what work was being done under his watch was admirable; unfortunately, what should have stopped at constructive challenges and asking probing questions turned into full-on interrogation and, eventually, insulting us as professionals.

Part of my job at the time was to maintain some technical engineering documents used as the foundation for the physical security plan at a nuclear power plant. Over several weeks, I had been reviewing and updating a set of diagrams when I began noticing discrepancies between the plant drawings and what I found in the plant itself. These documents were part of routine government inspections, so I was obligated to dig deeper. As I conducted my research, I would routinely throw on my hardhat and start walking down equipment, one pipe at a time, one valve at a time, and sometimes one tiny cable at a time.

One afternoon, while Bert was in his oversight

role, I had returned to my desk after a walk-down when a disturbance in the universe sent a chill down my spine. I pivoted in my chair to see Bert lurking on the threshold of my cubicle. "Richard, what have you been up to? I've noticed you've been away from your desk quite a bit the past few days," Bert said, his words dripping with accusation, and his face contorted into a smirk that made me want to say, "F*#k off, Bert!" Okay, that's not entirely accurate… it wasn't the smirk; I always wanted to tell Bert to f*#k off.

I swiveled in my chair, forced a half-hearted smile, and began to explain what I was doing and why, "Bert, I've been updating several drawings in preparation for next month's inspection. If I'm right about some of the things I found, we have some discrepancies that could be problematic if we don't address them. I've been meeting with engineering and..."

Bert interrupted me, "Wait, you found discrepancies," he asked in a doubtful tone while simultaneously checking his cell phone.

I subdued my frustration at being interrupted and replied in a way that would allow me to finish my explanation. "Yes, some things didn't add up, and I talked to folks in both Engineering and Operations to validate what I found..."

The dick interrupted me again, "You took this to Engineering and Operations? Why would you do that? Shouldn't someone more qualified be addressing this?" The tone that time was disgust with a side order of confusion. "What would <u>you</u> be able to tell <u>them,</u>" he asked smugly.

Most people would be pissed off at hearing something like that. Others would experience a sense of disbelief and perhaps awe that someone would have the audacity to be such a smug asshole, but this was Bert. Asshole was right on brand.

As I began to speak again, Bert flipped open his phone again to either check the time or look at a text, then put his hand out toward my face as if to shoosh me and, with that f--king smirk again, said, "You know what, I got it. You want to show that you're doing something, and you've found a crisis to solve. Let's hold off on distracting Operations with this."

Reflecting on it now, I don't know what bothered me more: his insulting words, his tone, the fact that he shooshed me like I was a f*#king child, or that he spoke at me while scrolling through his phone, never bothering to make eye contact while insulting me. Either way, the argument that followed was unproductive and a little on the unprofessional side, and then ended with Bert saying, "That's fine, I'll just speak with Will when he returns. In the meantime, I need you to put this on hold."

The next day, one of the engineers I'd been collaborating with found some documents that validated my suspicions. We went into Will's office, where Bert had set up shop, to bring it to his attention. He was reading and responding to emails. While we stood there, waiting patiently, he stared at the screen and mumbled, "Um yeah, go ahead." We began explaining what we had found; Bert failed to acknowledge a single word that was said or even look up at us as we pointed out markings on several plant drawings and read text from engineering change documents.

After a few minutes, I signaled to the engineer, and we simply stopped talking. Bert didn't notice for nearly a full minute and offered a halfhearted, "Um, okay, is that everything?"

The engineer just looked at me in disbelief. I asked, "Bert, did you hear the part about the drawings not matching what's installed?"

Bert took another 15 seconds or so to finish reading his email and said, "Yup, all good stuff." He got up from his chair and walked over to a small table in the office where we had spread out the drawings. With a swift glance, he said, "We're fine. I think we've all known about this stuff for a long time." With that, he began to walk out of the room while giving me a firm, condescending pat on the shoulder.

"Bert, I'm not trying to say this is a crisis; I am saying we need to address this." I blurted out quickly as I followed him out of the office.

Bert just gave me a thumbs up as he nodded his head with that stupid frown on his face that was supposed to say, "No worries," but actually said, "You're not important enough for my time." Bert didn't return to finish our discussion, and I refused to waste my time chasing him.

As it so happened, what I had discovered was a significant discrepancy. When Will returned, he took these findings seriously. In the year or so that followed,

I discovered several other discrepancies, several of which were significant. Bert was moved around from one position to the next and eventually demoted after his dick-ish leadership style had pissed off the right number of people.

One final piece to this tale, and not because it has to do with leadership, but because it just made me smile. Will had decided to give the staff an extra day off during one year's holiday. I don't recall the exact details, but I remember sitting beside Bert in the conference room when Will mentioned it.

Everyone was quite excited except Bert, who was reading through the pages of a policy. He leaned over to me and pointed to a line in the policy that would negate what Will was offering. Bert then said, "I'm gonna have to crush their spirits now. You see, this is what makes me the asshole."

I immediately replied with a heartfelt, "No, Bert, there is so much more that makes you an asshole."

Let's talk about all the ways Bert sucked.

Bert sucked in ways that historians and archeologists will be studying hundreds of years from now. For the sake of brevity, here are the top 3:

- Bert used his intelligence and attention to detail to be hyper-critical and belittled people instead of providing valuable feedback that people could appreciate and act on.
- Bert actively treated others as if his intellect made him superior (overt behaviors).
- Bert had a whole collection of subtle behaviors, like checking a watch or cell phone while people were talking and hand gestures like the quiet down or shooshing gesture. Those behaviors send not-so-subtle messages.

What does this mean to you?

I know what you're thinking, "how did this dick end up as a boss in the first place?" From what I know of his past, he was picked by other lousy bosses who only saw the traits they thought mattered and didn't know enough to evaluate different characteristics beyond intelligence and the ability to criticize. This pattern is far too common in the workplace. F*#%'d up bosses spin up other F*#%'d up bosses because they recognize familiar traits they share. The problem is, those traits ain't all good.

Bert had a critical eye, which is a good trait, but he didn't know how to give feedback without insulting. Not to intentionally overuse the word critical, but it is critically important to understand the difference between valuable critical feedback (also referred to as "value-added" critical feedback) and simple criticism for the sake of nit-picking.

Bert's explanations repeatedly failed to engage his audience, not just because he lacked talent as a speaker or presenter but his inability to connect with others. I've seen people's eyes glaze over when I got too technical or long-winded. I had to learn to shift my approach and reconnect, but Bert never did. He viewed those who couldn't follow his complex monologues as inferior. Such an approach indicates a leader who talks 'at' people, not with or to them, merely giving orders instead of genuinely connecting and communicating.

As we've read, personality can significantly influence a leader's impact. Overconfidence and egotism send messages so loudly that even the most positive messages can go unheard. Leaders must remember that they are not the message, only the messenger.

Key Takeaways

Critical doesn't mean asshole. Feedback, observations, and coaching are tools intended to provide help and support. These activities point out where someone can do better and, whenever possible, also show them how. Critical feedback should never target the person but instead focus on actions or behaviors. It's all about helping the person or team grow.

On the flip side, criticism (the favorite tool of the asshole boss) is often unclear, without offering clear steps for improvement, and can feel like a personal attack. Making people feel bad about themselves or their work is a great way to make them stop trying and make them see you as an adversary instead of an ally. The next time you provide feedback, ask yourself, "Is what I'm saying really going to help others improve, or am I just pointing out what's wrong to make me look smart?

Don't be the dumbest smart person. Brilliant people are still quite capable of being dumb as hell when interacting with others. Kindergarten teachers are much more educated than their students. Yet, they recognize that to connect with them, they must put their superior intellect to work and find the right tone, words, and expressions to communicate effectively. Talking over someone's head using "big words" can be distracting and off-putting. Don't use jargon or sound like you read the thesaurus every night before bed.

Speak to connect, not to impress. A leader's connection, empathy, and genuine care for their people are far more valuable than their intelligence. People won't appreciate your intellect if they can't get past your personality long enough to recognize it.

Subtle behaviors – aren't. Words are heard (or read) and interpreted by the brain to connect those words with a meaning. Behaviors, things that can be observed, also connect with meanings in our brains. Just imagine someone saying "yes" while shaking their heads from side to side. Subtle behaviors, such as checking your watch (look up highlights of the 1992 town hall presidential debate), hand gestures, or checking your phone, can be just as telling about your thoughts and feelings as facial expressions.

Not all subtle behaviors are bad. Nodding when you agree with something, deliberately putting your phone away, making eye contact, and turning completely away from your computer screen with your hands off the keyboard when someone is speaking to you are all subtle but still tell people that they are important enough to engage with and give your full attention to. In this new era of remote work, teleconferences (Zoom or Teams meetings without cameras) can erode our skills at interacting with people face to face. We don't need to worry about eye contact or have to hide our eye rolls. We can multi-task or pick out wedgies without fear of being insulting or distracting to others. Putting on your camera while not pressuring others to turn on theirs allows you to exercise these behaviors that send all the right messages.

CHAPTER 4

"Tom - the Global Everything"

Arrogant. Egotistical. Narcissistic. Manipulative. Autocratic. Pompous. Each of these traits individually can turn a boss into a horrible, no-good boss. What happens when you roll all of them into a single biomorphic entity? (That's a fancy way of saying something with the characteristics of a living organism - because I didn't feel that calling Tom a person was fair to actual people.) The answer is the most horriblist, no-goodest, lousiest, f*#%ing boss of all bosses. The "capo di tutti capi" in mafia terms. To highlight the level of egotism we're talking about here, this is the person who told his team that he was in charge of so much that he was the "Global Everything" (and you better believe that is all we referred to him as when we weren't using more colorful expletives).

Tom's dramatic rise up the corporate ladder was a spectacle of manipulation. Leadership abilities were ignored, and success wasn't defined by his team's growth and morale. The real irony was the upper management's infatuation with his immature theatrics, mistaking them for leadership qualities. They appeared to thrive on his forceful demeanor and loud over-confidence, believing it to be genuine leadership. Even with warnings of the toxic atmosphere he created, potential profit impacts held more weight than the people who actually did the work.

Part 1 - "People's Personal Bullshit"

One afternoon, I was working with Tom and a few other colleagues on a project in a small conference room. A brand-new employee knocked on the door and was waved in by Tom. The young man was there to confirm that, when he was hired a week earlier, they had agreed to his taking a few days of unpaid leave for some previously arranged family business. I immediately appreciated the employee recognizing that it was better to overcommunicate with his new boss than assume they were on the same page.

Rather than a simple thumbs up or genuine acknowledgment, Tom stuck his hand out at the young man and said, "Okay, stop! I don't have time for this. Fine, take the time off. Is there anything else?"

Without blinking an eye, the employee politely said, "No, nothing else, thank you," and walked out of the room.

The door shut, and Tom looked at those of us in the room in utter frustration, "I don't have time for people's personal bullshit." He shook his head and returned to focusing on his laptop screen.

Not sure how to take what I had just witnessed, I looked at my colleagues, who quickly broke eye contact and appeared to pretend that it didn't just happen. I excused myself from the room and tracked down the young man at his desk. I thanked him for being proactive while apologizing and making some weak excuses for the boss, but I suspected there was more to what I had just witnessed.

Part 2 - One Awe-Shit

While conducting an annual performance review for members of the team, Tom refused to grant a "meets expectations" rating because two weeks earlier, a team member failed to deliver an important presentation "on time." I quoted "on time" because Tom said he needed it "on Wednesday." What he later revealed was that he meant "by Wednesday." In a panic upon not finding the materials in his inbox Wednesday morning, Tom formed a so-called "crisis team" to complete this so-called urgent PowerPoint. Later, it was revealed that the team member was awaiting materials to finalize the presentation and would have delivered it by late Wednesday morning.

When I tried to reason with Tom, he kept returning to the same feeble argument, "He put me in crisis mode for a whole day; I can't give him 3%." For nearly 10 minutes, I attempted to explain that the employee had exceeded expectations for the entire year and had shown the most growth despite this one incident. I even offered to provide the documentation, but Tom was adamant and responded with, "Well, I don't know about any of that. All I see is the crisis he put me in."

Sarcastically, I asked if the policy was that 'one awe-shit wipes out a thousand atta-boys,' to which he responded, "That's right, if someone's gonna mess up, he better do it early in the year, so I forget about it."

That year, folks who appeared to be hand-picked by Tom received positive reviews, healthy raises, and a nice bonus, while others were given excuses.

Part 3 - "You're Brand Isn't Good Enough"

For a while, I worked closely with a "C" level executive in the organization, whom we'll refer to as Victor. Aware of my dissatisfaction under Tom's supervision, Victor asked if I might be interested in assuming leadership of a distinct department within the company. We had previously acknowledged this department's urgent need for reorganization, sharpened focus, and robust leadership. Interestingly, this was the same department Tom had suggested I should lead, albeit with the stipulation that I continue to report directly to him, thereby ensuring the department fell squarely under his control as part of his empire.

I was excited about the opportunity for a few reasons. First, it was a chance to escape Tom's tyranny. Second, I had a great deal of experience in that area and enjoyed that type of work. Most importantly, though, there was a great group of people who I'd be able to work with and build a highly effective and cohesive team.

Victor expressed concern that Tom would balk at the idea of taking me away from him because he'd have to figure out who else would take over my leadership role, which spanned several domains. As a result, Victor suggested that I keep this plan under wraps and develop a complete business plan that assured a smooth transition. When done, I was to pitch the idea and see how Tom responded.

Here are some things to keep in mind before I reveal how this whole thing turned out: First, under this new arrangement, I would no longer report to Tom. Instead, I would directly report to executive leadership without Tom filtering what they saw and heard from me. Second, Tom could no longer take credit for any of my or my team's accomplishments. Third, I would be influential in how certain portions of the company operate and have a potential voice in the company's future. If you've picked up anything about Tom thus far, I'm sure you already see why this idea had no chance of getting a warm reception.

Finally, it was time to share this idea with Tom. As I laid out the plan Victor and I had meticulously crafted, I couldn't ignore the visceral reaction on his face. It was a display of raw emotions – sheer disbelief and shock with a dash of disgust.

I had only gotten through the highlights when

Tom interrupted me with a barrage of insulting, intimidating, and expletive-laden comments. The most memorable amongst those comments included, "...your brand isn't f*#%ing good enough for a role like that. No, you need to stay where you are. I could do that job, but not you. You're not there yet." The remainder of the discussion was just more of the same, with Tom repeating himself and finding new ways to say the exact same thing, "no."

Victor, though somewhat taken aback, wasn't entirely shocked by Tom's explosive reaction. Even though Victor had the authority to make this happen without Tom's approval, this outburst was a clear indicator that moving forward would likely lead to unwanted drama and tension, leading him to drop the idea reluctantly. During my encounter with Victor, I waited patiently for him to address the behaviors I had been subject to at the hands of Tom. I repeated some of the things I was told and called, but Victor offered nothing more than a 'that's too bad.'

Unfortunately for me, that episode did not lead to any relief; it was quite the opposite, in fact. It served to alert Tom to the possibility that there could be a future for me out from under his iron grip, which didn't sit well at all. All that appeared to do was lead to the events of "Part 4" below.

Part 4 - "Only Through Me & You're Welcome"

A company senior executive, we'll call her Connie, had asked me to look into the details for implementing an internal program my team was uniquely qualified for. Over a period of three weeks or so, I proceeded to send the relevant information she requested. The following steps, however, required a decision from Connie, leading me to ping her through Microsoft Teams.

Weeks later, I received a call on my private cell from Tom, who opened with, "I don't want the company listening in on our conversation, so I'm calling you here." He told me that my name had come up in a conversation with "the exec-u-bots," and they were apparently very upset that I was reaching out to an executive team member, clearly trying to go behind his back. Tom claimed not to have any additional details but insisted that I stayed off the radar to save my job. He ended with, "Only talk to leadership through me."

Everything about that call seemed off. What made Tom think the company was listening in? Why would Connie complain about a handful of Teams messages when she had requested the information? What had I done that was so against policy or even etiquette that the executives were pissed off? Why did the call have to be so private that he couldn't risk anyone else hearing it?

When I pressed for details, Tom proceeded to inform me that he was told to fire me a long time ago but that he talked the executives out of it. Again, I begged for more information because the entire call was getting more and more bizarre. After nearly five minutes of hearing about how he rescued the department and saved my job without providing a single detail of my apparent terrible work, he punctuated it in his smug, asshole tone by saying, "You're welcome."

I was not sure where to turn, so I spoke to a representative from HR who offered condolences but offered little in terms of a path forward. I was told to document my interactions and to determine if I believed I was in a 'hostile work environment.' I did as the HR rep suggested but never actually escalated the situation.

When the opportunity presented itself, I still exchanged simple pleasantries with the company's senior executives but avoided discussions of any real importance. Several weeks passed, and a "C" level executive from out of town was visiting. He stopped by my office to say hello and asked the usual 'How are you?' 'It's good to see you' type of stuff. But as we continued to chat, he said the strangest thing, "I haven't heard much from you lately. You've been kind of distant."

By that time, I had heard enough back-channel communications from others in our department that Tom was talking about wanting me gone and trying to promise favors, even promotions, to those who would support him. With this in mind, I figured there was nothing left to lose, so I revealed what I had been told. The next half-hour turned out to be either a true revelation for this individual or some damn fine acting as he claimed to know nothing of the situation. Our little chat ended with this individual promising me that he would look into it personally and follow up with me soon.

Over the next several months, Tom made a series of maneuvers that diminished my overall role, and then, since he couldn't remove me for any performance issues, executed what he labeled a "reorganization" (a loophole that companies use to get rid of someone when they don't have a legitimate cause). By convincing the execs that eliminating my role (and only my role) was in the company's best interest, Tom got me out of his way and further ensured that the only narrative that ever left the department was his. Let's add fascism to the list of Tom's skills and attributes.

Here is just a random collection of more f*#%ed-up-ness worth sharing:

- Tom tried to get several of us to investigate the company's anonymous employee survey results in an effort to determine who had written what so that he could target them directly.
- Tom routinely undermined executive leadership, calling them 'exec-u-bots' and arguing that they were too dim to understand what we did. He claimed he had to simplify everything for their "simple executive brains."
- While speaking to some engineers, Tom once referred to all his employees who weren't engineers as "just a bunch of dopes." That got back to the team and immediately began deteriorating morale.

- To grow his empire within the company, Tom would routinely talk amongst his people about picking out weak leaders of other departments so he could try and take over their groups.
- Tom often discussed his strategy of fast talking over people and attacking them verbally until they "self-destructed" and just quit. I never saw it work, but I saw him attempt it several times.

Oddly enough, company leadership failed to recognize the cancer they were allowing and, by lack of intervention, enabled it to metastasize within the team. Tom was a quintessential horrible boss because he embodied the worst traits of our previous no-good, lousy f*#%ing bosses. Let's review:

- Miriam's Disdain for Personal Needs: Like Miriam, who ridiculed and shamed her employees for seeking guidance, Tom blatantly disregarded the personal aspects of his team's lives. He openly complained about "dealing with people's bullshit," showing a similar insensitivity to the fact that employees are human beings with individual needs and circumstances outside of work.

- Erik's Ego and Jealousy: Echoing Erik's behavior, Tom couldn't tolerate the idea of his subordinates receiving recognition or opportunities for advancement. He viewed his team's successes as threats to his status, reacting with pettiness and jealousy, much like Erik, who undermined and devalued his team to protect his own position.
- Bert's Disregard for Team Morale: Tom shared Bert's indifference to his team's morale. Bert's lack of concern for how his actions affected people was mirrored by Tom, who seemed oblivious or indifferent to the demoralizing effect of his leadership style. Like Bert, Tom's actions and words often deflated the team's enthusiasm and confidence, creating an environment where people felt undervalued and uninspired.

In combining these traits, Tom not only replicated the failures of Miriam, Erik, and Bert but also created a uniquely toxic leadership style that was detrimental to the morale and effectiveness of his team.

Let's talk about ~~all~~ *some* of the ways Tom sucked

Where to begin...

- Tom didn't see people, only resources. The needs of the individual were inconveniences that he couldn't be bothered with.
- Tom rewarded people according to how he felt and what aligned with his needs, not based on performance, growth, or merit. A single mistake could overshadow all accomplishments.
- Tom was jealous, petty, and controlling. Anything and anyone outside of his control was seen and often treated as a threat.
- Tom's ambition and desire for control and influence were unhealthy; he sowed disrespect to other organizational leaders, as well as those he was supposed to mentor.

What does this mean to you?

Now, let's unpack the carnival of chaos that is Tom's leadership style, or lack thereof. You've probably encountered a Tom at some point – the person who turns every workspace into a battlefield of egos. In the twisted world of Tom's leadership, it's a case study of what not to do.

Tom was obsessed with empire-building rather than team-building. Authentic leadership should foster a community, not expand one's dominion. Tom used to quip about having "dictator moments" and putting his foot down when he wanted his way. He failed to realize that leadership isn't a solo performance; it's an ensemble act.

Tom's leadership style was marred by pettiness, which was especially evident in performance reviews. He fixated on single incidents, overlooking a history of hard work, personal growth, and achievement. This approach not only demoralized team members but also eroded trust. Effective leadership requires recognizing and valuing effort, not focusing on momentary setbacks. Tom's inability to do so highlighted a lack of fairness, shortsightedness, and a narrow-minded perspective.

And let's talk about ego. Tom's story screams of ego run amok. An inflated ego can blind you to your team's needs. Leaders should seek to reinforce and nurture those around them, not focus on self-importance.

Lastly, fostering or enabling a toxic environment can be as simple as planting poisoned seeds amongst the team. When a leader is willing to engage in tearing down others, even those on their team, trust, and loyalty cannot grow. Expressions of raw ambition at the expense of others tell those around you that they will be sacrificed if necessary to achieve your goals.

So, don't be a Tom. Your responsibility is creating an environment where everyone can grow, not just the one in charge. Remember, your legacy as a leader will be defined not by how high you climbed but by how many people you lifted up along the way.

Key Takeaways

Empire Building Is Not Leadership: Empire building, and the pursuit of power and influence have nothing to do with being a leader and everything to do with feeding one's ambition. Amassing personal power and control is the exact opposite of your responsibility, cultivating a thriving environment for the team.

Mistakes Are Not the End of the World: People are fallible and will always make mistakes. People must feel comfortable sharing their shortcomings and errors in the interest of learning and improving. A single mistake should not overshadow a person's accomplishments. Balance and fairness are essential.

The Perils of Undermining Trust: Trust is fragile and can be damaged with even the slightest of missteps. When a leader frequently abuses the people's trust, the leader's words and deeds become empty gestures. A simple comment behind someone's back may seem like a harmless act, but those who hear it will never forget it.

The Toxic Ripple Effect: The toxic manager affects more than just morale; it can penetrate every facet of a company culture. Tolerating behaviors is the same as endorsing them. By permitting and promoting individuals with toxic behaviors, a company sends a message to the entire workforce. The toxic person becomes the example of what the company truly values - regardless of any words to the contrary.

Beware of Pettiness: The petty individual reveals a great deal about their character, often overshadowing those qualities that can lead to greatness. Unless the leader can resist the urge to respond with pettiness and remain focused on truly important issues, the team will struggle to stay focused as well. Petty matters will be seen as important and make dealing with complex issues nearly impossible.

CHAPTER 5

Let's Talk About You

As you've journeyed through the previous chapters of this book, you've also trekked through the hall of shame of horrible bosses and been introduced to an array of individuals whose traits and behaviors serve as stark examples of what to avoid in leadership. These narratives are more than mere stories; they are reflective tools for you to use on your own leadership journey. By recognizing and understanding the traits of ineffective leadership as portrayed by some of my lousy f*#%ing bosses, you can consciously avoid falling into similar patterns yourself.

If you have read this far (and didn't just skip to the end) and recognize some of yourself in these stories, it isn't too late to turn things around. In fact, reading this book all the way through could mean that you don't want to be a horrible boss but, instead, a true leader who inspires and uplifts those around you. Maybe your people think you're a horrible boss and sent you this book as a not-so-subtle hint. The good news is that you've already read the book. Now, take the next steps toward becoming a good leader. Of course, you could ignore the cues and the lessons from this book and never amount to anything more than a boss (and a lousy one at that). What you do next will impact what you will become - choose wisely.

Any insights from the earlier chapters should fuel your personal growth and development (or transformation if you are looking to turn things around). This chapter is about converting awareness into action. Ensuring that the leader you are in reality aligns with the leader you aspire to be (provided that leader isn't actually a dick).

Let's be honest: telling stories and throwing a bunch of key takeaways at you isn't enough. I'm very aware that most people won't take the time to perform self-assessments, keep journals, or gather anonymous survey results from their folks. Therefore, let's approach the next steps a bit differently. Let's start with a question.

Are you sure you're ready for this?

Don't be so quick to answer that. It isn't a trick question, but the word "ready" is a bit loaded.

As you reflect on your path forward, it's crucial to think long and hard about whether or not you are ready to be something more than just a boss. This may surprise you (or not if this applies to you), but some people are perfectly fine with being nothing more than a boss. They thrive on having power and influence or, as Tom often said, "being in command." Some people covet positions of power because they can easily shift focus away from their own failings to place blame on their people.

Leadership, in its most effective form, requires a selfless approach, putting the needs and growth of others before your own personal accolades. This journey is about being more than just a boss; it's about being a true leader who nurtures and elevates those around them. If you are not willing to practice what Captain Mike used to call "Big U, little I," be honest with yourself, and don't make victims of others simply to fulfill your needs.

Ask yourself these challenging questions:

- Am I willing to set my ego aside to give others credit, even when not all the credit is theirs? Would I develop a good idea and give the team credit for it to help boost morale? Leaders should be less focused on claiming victories and more on creating an environment where victories can happen, thanks to your team's contributions.

- Can I step away from the spotlight to ensure there is room for others to shine? Sometimes, the most impactful leadership move is to step back and let your team take the lead, allowing them to grow and be recognized for their efforts.
- Am I prepared to brag about my team's achievements without using it as an opportunity to boost my brand? True leaders take pride in their team's accomplishments and freely share these successes with others, highlighting the team's talents rather than their own.

These considerations are not merely rhetorical questions but challenges that you, as a leader, must be willing to embrace. It's about shifting the focus from 'I' to 'We.' It means celebrating the successes of other individuals or as a collective achievement and seeing your team's growth as a reflection of effective leadership.

Incorporating these aspects into your leadership style requires commitment and a genuine willingness to prioritize the development and success of your team above personal gain. This approach fosters a positive and productive work environment and cultivates a legacy of respected and admired leadership.

Remember, becoming a great leader involves many steps – some small, some significant. Each action you take towards putting your team first, acknowledging their efforts, and fostering their growth brings you closer to being the leader your people genuinely deserve. So, as you proceed, consider these challenges as integral milestones in your leadership journey, shaping not just your professional persona but also the lives and careers of those you lead.

Stop Talking About Leading - Start Leading

So, what's the next practical step? It's about creating an actionable plan tailored to your unique leadership journey. Fear not; becoming a better leader isn't about performing a complete overhaul overnight. It's about making small, consistent changes that accumulate over time. Arnold Schwarzenegger became Mr. Olympia one day, one exercise, and one lift at a time - think about that.

Start Small, But Start Now: Pick one or two

traits or behaviors you've recognized and focus on improving them. It could be something as simple as ensuring you listen more in meetings or acknowledging the contributions of your team members more frequently.

Engage in Honest Conversations: Initiate open discussions with your team. You don't have to ask outright if they think you're a horrible boss – instead, ask for their input on how the group can work better together and how you can be more supportive. This can provide indirect insights into your leadership style.

Set Clear, Achievable Goals: Based on your self-reflection, set specific goals for yourself. These goals should be realistic and measurable. For instance, commit to pointing out an accomplishment or positive trait for at least 5 members of your team, and do your best to make the feedback public. Do this often enough, and you will become an expert at seeing the best in people - an essential and achievable.

Seek Out Mentors or Coaches: Find someone whose leadership style you admire, either within your organization or outside it. A mentor or coach can provide invaluable advice, guidance, and an external perspective. If your pride still won't allow you to get help, start small, read, watch videos, or do whatever you need to do to find a model you can emulate. If you're doing it right, you'll eventually be willing to set your ego aside and engage directly. Since this is a behavior you want your folks to be able to emulate, you better learn it yourself.

Reflect Regularly: Make it a habit to reflect on your day or week. What went well in terms of your leadership? What could have been better? This regular reflection can help you stay aware and focused on your leadership journey. The most important thing during any reflection is to avoid sensationalizing your experiences or allowing yourself to make excuses. Be honest with yourself about your day or week's progress. Own it, good or bad. If you didn't do well, identify why and commit to improving.

Embrace Feedback: Actively seek feedback, not just from your team but from peers and superiors as well. Be open to this feedback, even if it's hard to hear. The ability to seek out and accept critical feedback will teach those around you that feedback is an opportunity, not an attack. What follows is open and honest discord across all levels of your team. The most effective teams can engage in healthy debate and survive the clashing of ideas.

Celebrate Small Wins: Recognize and celebrate progress in your leadership journey. This could be as simple as a team member expressing appreciation for your support or someone implementing a personal change you suggested. If someone notices that you are doing something well as a leader, it's like being asked if you've been working out - they recognize a difference, and it was enough to make them bring it up. Since leadership is ultimately made up of many little things, small wins - aren't actually small at all.

How will you know when you are making progress?

After you've performed those seven leadership exercises for about 30 to 60 days, something pretty incredible will come into focus. You'll realize that you've not just been focusing on good leadership; you've been practicing it and modeling it for your people as well. You don't have to be a great leader tomorrow; just be better today. (And if you're a horrible boss, just be less of a lousy f*#%ing boss each day.) Eventually, you won't just be measuring your achievements as a leader; you'll be measuring the achievements and growth of the leaders you create around you - and those are the achievements that will matter most.

ACKNOWLEDGEMENTS

Without others, there is no one to provide us with guidance, inspiration, and correction, or, to provide leadership to.

Numerous individuals have coached and mentored me along my leadership journey, tolerating my often-steep learning curve, and never tolerating excuses, or less than I was capable of.

I'm truly grateful first and foremost to my family and friends who, despite the multiple promises of a finished book, never wavered in their patience, belief, and support.

Thank you to my wife who had every reason to doubt me, but kept believing. My children, Alexandra, Madison, Adam, and Jacob, for always loving and never judging. My parents for modeling goodness and teaching me to believe in myself, and my siblings for their unrelenting encouragement and prayers.

To Captain Mike Redding, the model of a good man, good friend, and great leader.

AFTERWORD

As we close the pages of "Horrible, No-Good, Lousy, F*#%ing Bosses and How Not to Be One," it's essential to take a moment to reflect on the journey we've taken together. This book wasn't just a showcase of managerial nightmares but a stark reminder of how to not lead. It was a mirror held up to the realities of management and a guide to avoiding the pitfalls of poor leadership. From Miriam's disregard for empathy to Erik's ego-driven antics and Bert's critical nature to Tom's self-centered ambition, each story serves as a lesson in how bad bosses murder morale and terrorize their teams. But beyond these stories, this book was a call to introspection – an invitation to examine your leadership style and behaviors.

If you embrace the things you've learned here, I promise, you can become the kind of leader people want to follow. I know it's true, not because I've seen it, but because I've lived it. I was once a lousy boss who cared more about getting the job done than caring for those who relied on me. It took real leaders, like Captain Mike and many others, to mold, guide, and help me see that being a leader was more than titles, tasks, and objectives; it was about people above all else.

The Power of Positive Leadership: While the focus of this book has been on what not to do, it's equally important to recognize the power of positive leadership. Similar to looking at life with a glass-half-empty or glass-half-full perspective, positive leadership means keeping the team's focus on achievement, growth, and learning opportunities rather than focusing on the negative. It is far too easy to get caught in the traps of complaining, criticizing, and even placing blame. Once headed down that path, the leader can end up forging a path toward negativity, a place entirely unsuitable for building people up, improving performance, and enhancing morale.

Change - Not Just a Buzzword: Change is not just a trendy buzzword tossed around at leadership seminars; it's one of the most essential activities of a team and critical skills a leader can have. Improving at anything means change, whether it's being more supportive and available to your people, becoming a better listener, or learning how to accept and apply critical feedback. Equally crucial to accepting change is driving it. Pushing people to grow and move beyond their comfort zones is the leader's obligation. Fostering continual improvement without creating a "never good enough" environment requires a steady hand, clear vision, and constant oversight. Once complacency begins to set in, things change for the worse. Switching up a strategy, tactic, or structure in order to keep things moving forward is exactly the kind of change a leader must be ready to initiate - the leader is the agent of change.

What Not to Be: If you've seen glimpses of yourself in these stories, it's time to steer clear of the paths laid by our notorious examples. You don't want to be the next Tom or Erik, remembered for all the wrong reasons and nothing more than the punchline of people's jokes. Transform your leadership style from being a nightmare to being a force of positive change. Look in the mirror and ask, "Am I the reason my people hate Mondays?"

In conclusion, as you close this book, remember that you have a chance to make a real difference in people's lives. Avoid becoming a chapter in "Lousy, F*#%ing Bosses Part II." Strive to be the leader who's respected, not just tolerated; admired, not feared. May your leadership journey be one of growth, empathy, and positive influence, steering clear of the traps that turned our infamous bosses into cautionary tales.

If you got a kick out of this book, found some wisdom in

its pages, or just had a few good laughs, recommend it to a friend, send them one as a gift, or send a loud message to a lousy boss. Head over to our website at **www.bigbookofbadbosses.com**.

Big Book of Bad Bosses is more than just a website; it's a growing community. And who knows, if you share a tale that packs the right punch, you might hear from us looking for contributions for the sequel to this book.

Horrible, No-Good, Lousy, F*#%ing Bosses…

www.bigbookofbadbosses.com

The End

(…of this book, because so long as there are bad bosses in the world, we will keep writing and exposing their lousiness and sharing stories and calling them out for all of the rotten horrible bullshit they put us through and sending them copies of this book with inscriptions like "hey asshole, they wrote a book about you" or "keep it up and your name will be chapter 1 of the next book you sonofabitch". You get the point.)

www.ingramcontent.com/pod-product-compliance
Lightning Source LLC
Chambersburg PA
CBHW050234230526
45470CB00005B/1952